Close Reading Companion

Mc
Graw
Hill
Education

Cover and Title pages: Nathan Love

www.mheonline.com/readingwonders

Send all inquiries to:
McGraw-Hill Education
Two Penn Plaza
New York, New York 10121

ISBN: 978-0-02-130746-3
MHID: 0-02-130746-6

Printed in the United States of America.

13 LMN 22

E

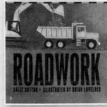

The Animal Kingdom

From Here to There

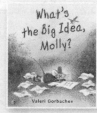

What About Bear?

COLLABORATE

? **Listen** Which words help you know how Bear feels when he can't play checkers? Draw clues.

Literature Big Book

Read Together

CLOSE READING

Tip of the Week

Hector

When I **reread**, I read carefully to make sure I understand.

Bear feels

_____

_ _

_____

Ken Cavanagh/McGraw-Hill Education

? **Look** How do Bear's feelings change when Goose and Fox play without him? Draw how Bear feels.

Bear's feelings changed from

_____

- -

"How to Be a Friend"

? **Find Clues** **How do the friends find ways to get along? Circle clues.**

Here are some ways
to get along.

1. Listen.

2. Share.

3. Play fair.

The friends

_____

- -

_____

Ken Cavanagh/McGraw-Hill Education

COLLABORATE

Look What are the friends doing? This art shows friends at a community event. Circle what they are doing.

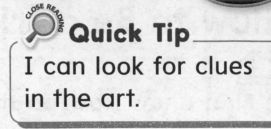

Quick Tip
I can look for clues in the art.

ImageZoo/SuperStock

Friends can

_____

- -

_____

Pouch!

COLLABORATE

? **Look** How does the illustrator help you know that Joey is talking? Draw a picture of what Joey wants to do.

Literature Big Book

CLOSE READING

Tip of the Week

Katie

When I **reread**, I look closely at the words.

Joey says he wants to

_____

- - - - - - - - - - - - - - - -

_____

COLLABORATE

? **Look** **What do the baby kangaroos want to do when they both say "No, thanks"? Draw the answer.**

The baby kangaroos both want to

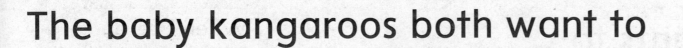

"Baby Animals on the Move!"

? **Find Clues** How do the people watch the birds move across the sky? Circle the clues.

People can watch animals

_____

- -

_____

(bkgd) Sean Duan/Moment/Getty Images; (inset) ©Randy Faris/Corbis

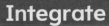

Listen How does the little bird move? Circle the words that tell you.

Quick Tip
I can make pictures in my mind.

The Little Bird

Once I saw a little bird
Come hop, hop, hop;
So I cried, "Little bird,
Will you stop, stop, stop?"

And was going
to the window
To say, "How do you do?"
But he shook his little tail,
And far away he flew.

Mark Dierker/McGraw-Hill Education

Baby animals can

_____

- -

_____

Senses at the Seashore

COLLABORATE

? **Look** How do senses help you know what the seashore is like? Draw clues here.

Literature Big Book

see	
hear	

Sappington Todd/Getty Images

Senses help me

_____

- -

_____

CLOSE READING

Tip of the Week

Kim

As I reread, I look at the photos to help me understand.

COLLABORATE

? **Listen** **What do the photos and words tell about seaweed? Draw or write about it.**

The seaweed is

_____

- -

_____

"I Smell Springtime"

Find Clues Which sense tells the girl that spring is here? Draw how she uses her senses.

Illustration: Kathleen Kemly

Spring is here because

_____

- -

_____

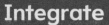

Look **How can you learn about the flowers? Write or draw what you can see, smell, and touch.**

Quick Tip
I can use my senses.

See	
Smell	
Touch	

Rijksmuseum, Amsterdam

My senses help me

_____

- -

_____

The Handiest Things in the World

COLLABORATE

? **Look** What is something that is the same in both photographs and something that is different? Draw what is different.

CLOSE READING

Tip of the Week

Logan

When I **reread**, I compare the pictures.

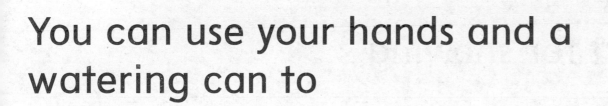

You can use your hands and a watering can to

_____

- -

_____

eurobanks/Shutterstock

COLLABORATE

? **Look** What is the hand handiest for showing?
Draw it.

The hand is handiest for showing

"Discover with Tools"

COLLABORATE

? **Find Clues** How do these pages compare what tools can do? Circle clues.

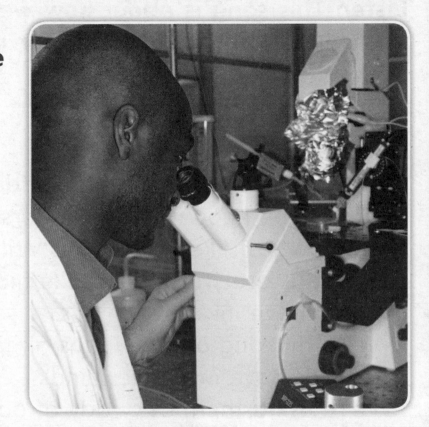

These tools find

_____

- -

_____

These tools find

_____

- -

_____

(l) Richard T. Nowitz/Science Source; (c) Cupak/mauritius images/age fotostock; (r) Noel Hendrickson/Photodisc/Getty Images

Listen This song is about how we use our minds to invent. What is your idea for an invention? Draw the tools you need.

CLOSE READING
Quick Tip
I think about the tools I need to invent or explore.

Inventive Minds

Inventions can change the world, you may say.
But did you know we're inventors today?
And now just like Orville and Wilbur Wright,
Our ideas are starting to take flight!
We all have inventive minds.
We're thinking of new ideas all the time.
Yes, kids have inventive minds.
We're using them ev'ry day of our lives!

I can make an invention with

_____

- -

Shapes All Around

Literature Big Book

? **Look** Which things in the pictures have you seen? Draw them.

CLOSE READING

Tip of the Week

Maria

When I **reread**, I look at the photographs.

I see squares in

_____

- -

_____

COLLABORATE

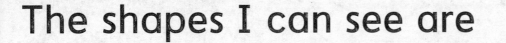

Look What shapes are at the end of the selection? Work with a partner to name them. Draw the shapes.

The shapes I can see are

"Find the Shapes"

COLLABORATE

? **Find Clues** Which thing is different from the others in its group? Circle it.

A thing that is soft is

_____

- - - - - - - - - - - - - - - - - - -

_____

A thing with flat sides is

_____

- -

_____

(tl) Creative Crop/Digital Vision/Getty Images; (tr) Ken Cavanagh/McGraw-Hill Education; (cr) C Squared Studios/Photodisc/Getty Images; (cr) Brian Hagiwara/Stockbyte/Getty Images; (bl) Dorling Kindersley/Getty Images; (br) George Diebold/Photodisc/Getty Images;

COLLABORATE

Look Which shapes are in the photo? Circle two shapes that can make a new shape. Draw the new shape.

CLOSE READING

Quick Tip
I can think about the shapes I see.

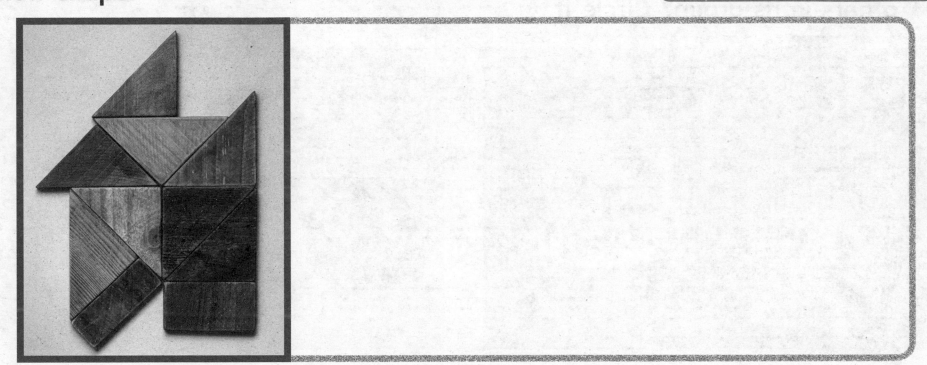

supermimicry/iStock/Getty Images

I see a square when I look at

I Love Bugs!

COLLABORATE

? **Look** Why do you think *I Love Bugs!* is a good title for this story? Draw clues here.

Literature Big Book

Read Together

Visage/Stockbyte/Getty Images

The story is about

_____

- -

_____

CLOSE READING

Tip of the Week

Yasmin

When I reread, I look for clues.

Listen How do the words help you learn about bugs in a fun way? Discuss with a partner. Draw bugs that the words describe.

The words about bugs are

_____

- -

_____

"Bugs All Around"

COLLABORATE

? Find Clues How does the photograph help you understand it is not safe to touch bugs? Circle the clues.

Do not touch the

_____

- - - - - - - - - - - - - - - - - - - -

_____

COLLABORATE

Look **What bugs do you see? Why does the man wear special clothes? Circle the special clothing.**

©Monty Rakusen/cultura/Corbis

A beekeeper gathers honey from a beehive.

The beekeeper has special clothing

_____

- -

_____

How Do Dinosaurs Go to School?

? **Listen** Is the dinosaur following the rules?
Draw clues here.

Literature Big Book

CLOSE READING

Tip of the Week

Leo

When I **reread**, I make pictures in my mind.

The dinosaur is

_____

- - - - - - - - - - - - - - - - - - - -

_____

©DreamPictures/Vanessa Gavalya/Blend Images/Corbis

Look How is the dinosaur's behavior different now? Draw what he is doing.

Now the dinosaur is

_____

- -

_____

"Be Safe!"

COLLABORATE

? **Find Clues** What rules and laws do the children follow? Circle the clues.

The children

_____

- - - - - - - - - - - - - - - - - - -

_____

The boy

_____

- - - - - - - - - - - - - - - - - - -

_____

Unit 3 • Week I • Rules to Go By **27**

COLLABORATE

Look Talk with a partner about what rules the children follow. Draw it.

CLOSE READING

Quick Tip

I think about which rules to follow in different places.

Rule

Children at a neighborhood lemonade stand.

A rule the children follow is

Clang! Clang! Beep! Beep! Listen to the City

COLLABORATE

? Look Why are some sound words big and some small? Draw a big or small sound.

This picture shows

_____

- -

_____

McGraw-Hill Education

Literature Big Book

CLOSE READING

Tip of the Week

Amelia

I look at the way the words are made when I **reread**.

? **Listen** How do the words and pictures show sounds at this time of day? Draw clues.

The pictures and words show

_____

- -

_____

"Sounds Are Everywhere"

COLLABORATE

? **Find Clues** What sounds do you hear?
Circle the instruments that make the sounds.

Hands beat on the drums and make the drums vibrate.

Boom, bang, boom are sounds made by

_____

- - - - - - - - - - - - - - - - - - - -

_____

Rah, dah, doo are sounds made by

_____

- - - - - - - - - - - - - - - - - - - -

_____

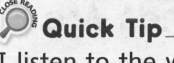

Listen Which words in the nursery rhyme have the same ending sounds? Talk about the words with a partner. Circle them.

Quick Tip
I listen to the words and how they sound.

As I Was Going Along

As I was going
along, along,
A-singing a comical
song, song, song,
The lane that I
went was so
long, long, long,

And the song that
I sang was so
long, long, long,
And so I went
singing along.

Words with the same ending sounds are

_____

- -

_____

Please Take Me for a Walk

COLLABORATE

? **Look** How do you know what the dog wants? Tell a partner. Draw one of the places.

Literature Big Book

Read Together

CLOSE READING

Tip of the Week

Sara

When I **reread**, I share ideas.

The words and pictures tell me

_____

- -

_____

sam74100/iStock/Getty Images Plus/Getty Images

? **Look** How do the dog's feelings change on these pages? Draw clues to show how the dog feels.

Page 24	Page 25

The dog feels

_____

- - - - - - - - - - - - - - -

_____

The dog feels

_____

- - - - - - - - - - - - - - - - - -

_____

"A Neighborhood"

? **Find Clues** What is in the library? Talk about it with a partner. Circle clues.

Library

The library has

_____

- -

_____

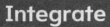

Look **What can you get at the farmer's market? Circle clues. Draw other things you can find there.**

🔍 **Quick Tip**

I can look for clues in in the art.

At the farmer's market, I can get

_____

- -

_____

Whose Shoes?

? **Look** What clues tell you why the boy is wearing boots? Draw the clues.

Hola Images/Getty Images

Tip of the Week

Michael

When I **reread**, I look at the photos for clues.

The boy wears boots because

_____

- -

_____

? **Look** **How is the text on these pages different from the text at the beginning of the story? Circle yes or no to answer the questions.**

How is the text different?

I. Is it bigger?	yes	no
2. Does it ask questions?	yes	no
3. Is it smaller?	yes	no

The text and photos help me find

_____

- -

_____

"Workers and Their Tools"

COLLABORATE

? **Find Clues** How do the small photos help show what the worker does? Circle the clues.

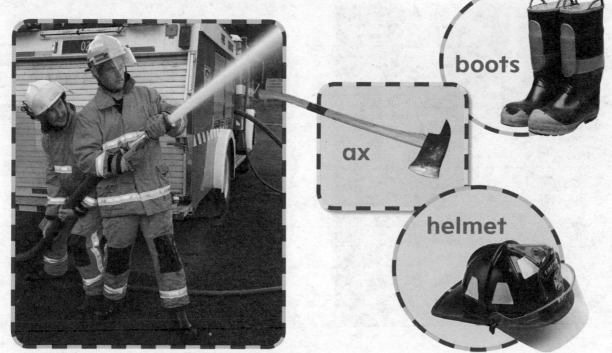

boots

ax

helmet

The small photos help because

_____

- -

_____

(l) Manchan/Photodisc/Getty Images; (tr cr br) Siede Preis/Photodisc/Getty Images

Look What is this man's job? What is he making? Circle the clues. Talk with a partner about how the man uses the tools. Draw a tool.

Quick Tip
I can look closely at the photo for clues.

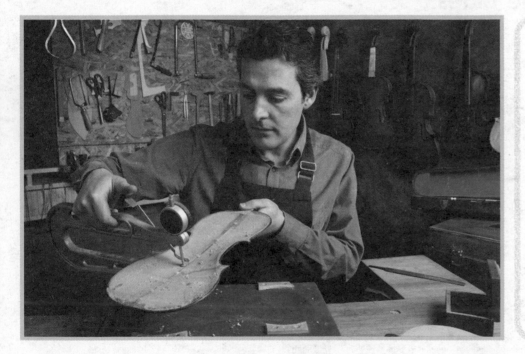

syolacan/E+/Getty Images

The man uses tools to make a

_____

- -

_____

What Can You Do With a Paleta?

COLLABORATE

? Listen **Which words help you know what the neighborhood is like? Draw it.**

Literature Big Book

CLOSE READING

Tip of the Week

Emma

When I **reread**, I look for clues.

In the neighborhood you can

Tetra Images-Mike Kemp/Getty Images

? Look How does the girl feel about the paleta?
Draw clues here.

The girl likes to

_____

- -

_____

"A World Festival"

COLLABORATE

? **Find Clues** How do Kyla's feelings change?
Circle clues.

Illustration: Mike Reed

Kyla feels that

_____

- -

_____

Kyla now feels

_____

- -

_____

Listen **This is a Japanese song. What are the friends doing? Circle it.**

Se, Se, Se

say say say
noh yoy yoy yo
oh chah lah kah
oh chah lah kah
oh chah lah kah hoy

oh chah lah kah
oh chah lah kah
oh chah lah kah hoy

Realistic Reflections

Friends can

_____

- -

_____

Roadwork

Listen Which words tell the sounds? Draw the machines. Write the sound words.

rubberball/Getty Images

The machines make the sounds

_____

- -

_____

Read Together

Literature Big Book

CLOSE READING

Tip of the Week

Ben

I look at sound words when I **reread**.

COLLABORATE

Look How do the words *sploshy, splashy,* and *splishy* help you know what the workers do? Draw it.

The words tell about the sound of

"A Community Garden"

COLLABORATE

? **Listen** Which words help you know the order of each step? Circle the words.

First, they dig.
Next, they plant seeds.
Then, they water.

The words tell

_____

- -

_____

(l) Jupiterimages/Photolibrary/Getty Images; (r) Noah Clayton/Photodisc/Getty Images

Integrate

Read Together

Look How do the people in the photo make the community better? Draw how they are helping.

Quick Tip
I can find clues in the photos.

JUPITERIMAGES/Brand X/Alamy

We make a community better by

_____

- -

_____

My Garden

COLLABORATE

? **Listen** What is real and what is not real in the garden? Draw it. Make a label.

MY GARDEN
KEVIN HENKES

Literature Big Book

Read Together

CLOSE READING

Tip of the Week

Amanda

When I **reread**, I look at the pictures.

My picture is

_____

- -

_____

Andreas Rodriguez/iStock/Getty Images Plus/Getty Images

? **Look** How does the author help you imagine flowers and strawberries at night? Draw it.

The flowers and strawberries look like

_____

- -

_____

"Tommy"

COLLABORATE

? **Listen** How does the boy feel at the end of the poem? Draw the clues and write a word.

The boy is surprised to see

_____

- -

_____

Listen **What might grow in Mary's garden or in the garden in the story *My Garden*? Draw it.**

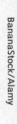

Quick Tip
I can compare the two texts.

Mary, Mary Quite Contrary

Mary, Mary, quite contrary,
How does your garden grow?
Silver bells and cockle-shells,
And pretty maids all in a row.

In a real garden

A Grand Old Tree

? **Listen** What words does the author use to make the tree seem like a person? Write the words.

The tree is like a person because

_____

- -

_____

Literature Big Book

CLOSE READING

Tip of the Week

Charlie

When I **reread**, I look for details about the tree.

 COLLABORATE

? **Look** **Why does the author put the words on the page this way? Draw the tree. Make a label.**

The words help me think about

_____

- -

_____

Read Together

"From a Seed to a Tree"

COLLABORATE

? **Find the Clue** What can you learn about apple seeds from the photograph? Circle the clue.

(l) John Foxx/Stockbyte/Getty Images; (r) Claire Higgins/Photolibrary/Getty Images

Apple seeds

_____

- -

_____

Read Together

Look What can you learn from the photo and caption? Tell a partner. How old was this tree? Write it.

CLOSE READING
Quick Tip
I can look for details about a tree.

Imagemore/Glow Images

This photo shows rings, or circles in a tree stump. Some trees grow one ring each year.

When I look at the photo, I learn

_____

- -

_____

An Orange in January

? **Look** How does the picture tell what the trip was like? Draw one place from the trip.

Literature Big Book

The trip was

_____

- -

_____

Steve Debenport/iStock/Getty Images Plus/Getty Images

CLOSE READING

Tip of the Week

Pedro

When I **reread**, the pictures help me understand.

COLLABORATE

? **Look** What other things in the picture are "bursting with the seasons inside" like the orange? Draw them. Make labels.

The orange is bursting with the seasons of

_____

- -

_____

"Farmers' Market"

COLLABORATE

? **Find Clues** What do the pictures tell you about how close or far farmers sell their foods? Circle clues.

Farmers sell food

(l) JMichi/iStock/Getty Images Plus/Getty Images; (tc) James Lauritz/Photodisc/Getty Images; (tr) Eric Taylor/Bloomberg via Getty Images; (br) Jill Braaten/McGraw-Hill Education

Look How is this farm the same and different from the farm in *An Orange in January?* Draw or write how they are the same and different.

CLOSE READING **Quick Tip**

I can compare illustrations.

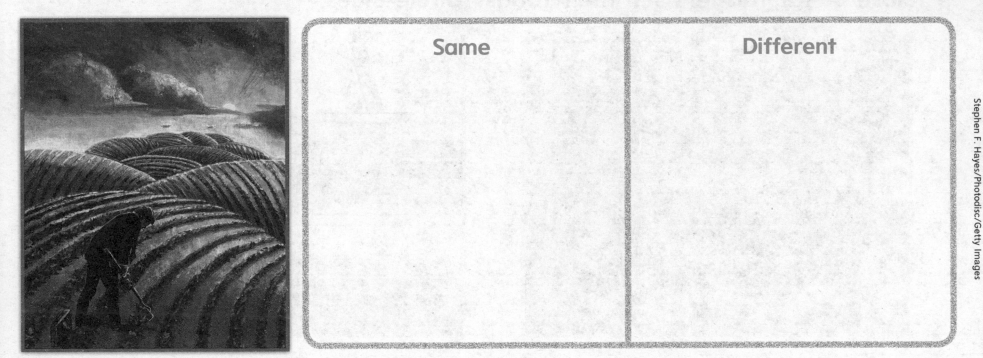

Same	Different

Stephen F. Hayes/Photodisc/Getty Images

Farms grow

_____

_____

Mama, Is It Summer Yet?

COLLABORATE

? **Look** How do the words and pictures show what season it is? Draw or list clues.

Literature Big Book

Read Together

[drawing box]

When trees bloom, it is

_____

- -

_____

Olena_T/iStock/Getty Images

CLOSE READING

Tip of the Week

Zoe

I look for clues in the words and pictures when I **reread**.

COLLABORATE

? **Listen** Which words help you know what summer is like? Draw it.

Summer is

_____

- -

_____

"Honey, I Love"

? **Find Clues** What words help tell what the poet loves about summer? Write the words. Draw a picture.

Words	Picture

The poet loves

_____

COLLABORATE

Look What clues in the art let you know what season it is? Draw or write the clues.

image courtesy National Gallery of Art

I know the season is

Rain

Literature Big Book

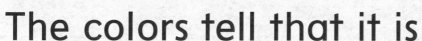

? Look **How do the colors help you think about the weather? Draw the picture. Make labels for *red, yellow* and *gray*.**

The colors tell that it is

_____

- -

_____

Read Together

CLOSE READING

Tip of the Week

Luis

When I **reread**, I think about how the author uses color.

COLLABORATE

Read Together

Listen **Which words help you think about the rain? Write them.**

I know that the rain is

_____

- -

_____

"Cloud Watch"

Find Clues How does the author tell about the weather? Circle the clues.

On Tuesday, there is

_____

_____

On Wednesday, there is

_____

_____

(l) Alan Marsh/Design Pics; (r) Natural Selection John Bracchi/Design Pics

Look What does this photo tell you about the weather? Write or draw the clues.

Quick Tip

I can use clues to tell about the weather.

Ariel Skelley/Blend Images LLC

On a summer day the weather is

_____

- -

Waiting Out the Storm

COLLABORATE

? **Listen** What do you picture in your mind when you hear the words about the rain? Draw it.

Ariel Skelley/Blend Images/Getty Images

The words tell about

_____

- -

_____

Literature Big Book

CLOSE READING

Tip of the Week

Paula

When I **reread**, I make pictures in my mind.

Read Together

COLLABORATE

? **Look How does the girl feel about the storm now? Draw clues here.**

The girl feels

70 Unit 6 • Week 3 • Stormy Weather

Read Together

"Be Safe in Bad Weather"

COLLABORATE

? **Find Clues** What words does the author use to tell that bad weather is on its way? Circle the words.

Whoosh! In some places strong winds blow in spring, summer, and fall.

Boom! How can you keep safe if you see lightning or hear thunder?

(l) Adam Burn/Getty Images; (r) Ingram Publishing/age fotostock

Whoosh! is the sound of

_____

- - - - - - - - - - - - - - - - - -

_____

Boom! is the sound of

_____

- - - - - - - - - - - - - - - - - -

_____

Look Circle how the family is staying safe and warm. Draw what might the weather be outside.

🔍 **Quick Tip**
I can make connections.

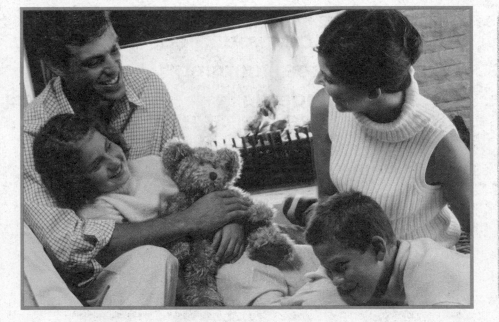

Goodshoot/Getty Images Plus/Getty Images

In very cold weather, stay safe by

_____

- -

_____

ZooBorns!

COLLABORATE

? **Listen** What animal does Kai look like? Draw it. Now draw the animal related to Kai.

Literature Big Book

Read Together

Kai Looks Like	Kai Is Related To

3sbworld/iStock/Getty Images

A hyena is related to a

_____

CLOSE READING

Tip of the Week

Steve

When I **reread**, I look at how the pictures and words match.

COLLABORATE

Read Together

? **Look** **How does the photo teach you about the ocelot? Circle the words that describe it. Then draw a pet that looks like an ocelot.**

An ocelot has _____.

whiskers   a shell

soft fur   a pink nose

feathers

The baby ocelot looks like a

_____

- -

_____

Read Together

"Kitty Caught a Caterpillar"

COLLABORATE

? Find Clues How do the pictures help you understand what Kitty could not do? Draw it.

Kitty could not

_____

- -

_____

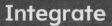

Look Circle two animals. Write one way they are the same. Write one way they are different.

Quick Tip
I look for what is alike and different.

Dorling Kindersley/Getty Images

Same	Different

These animals both

_____

- - - - - - - - - - - - - - - - - -

_____

The Birthday Pet

COLLABORATE

? **Listen** What rhyming word does the author use to predict Danny's next pet? Draw the pet.

Literature Big Book

Nga Nguyen/Moment/Getty Images

Danny's next pet is a

_____

- -

_____

CLOSE READING

Tip of the Week

Lucas

I think about rhyming words as I **reread**.

? Look How does Danny feel about his pet turtle? Draw and label a picture.

Danny feels

_____

- -

_____

"The Perfect Pet"

? Find the Clue How does the picture help you know why the girls name their pet *Racer*? Circle the clue.

The hamster's name is *Racer* because

_____

- -

_____

COLLABORATE

Look How does the girl feel about her rabbit?
Circle clues. Write words that tell how she feels.

Claudia Rehm, Red Chopsticks Images/Getty Images

Pets make us feel

_____

- -

_____

Bear Snores On

? **Listen** Which words show that the events in the cave began quietly? Circle the words. Draw a picture.

tip-toe

fluff-cold

cave

pitter-pat

squeaks

lights

damp

Words that show it is quiet are

_____

- -

_____

CLOSE READING

Tip of the Week

Kelly

When I **reread**, I look for word clues.

Jupiterimages/Stockbyte/Getty Images

COLLABORATE

? Listen **What story pattern do you notice?**
**What changes inside the cave? What stays
the same?**

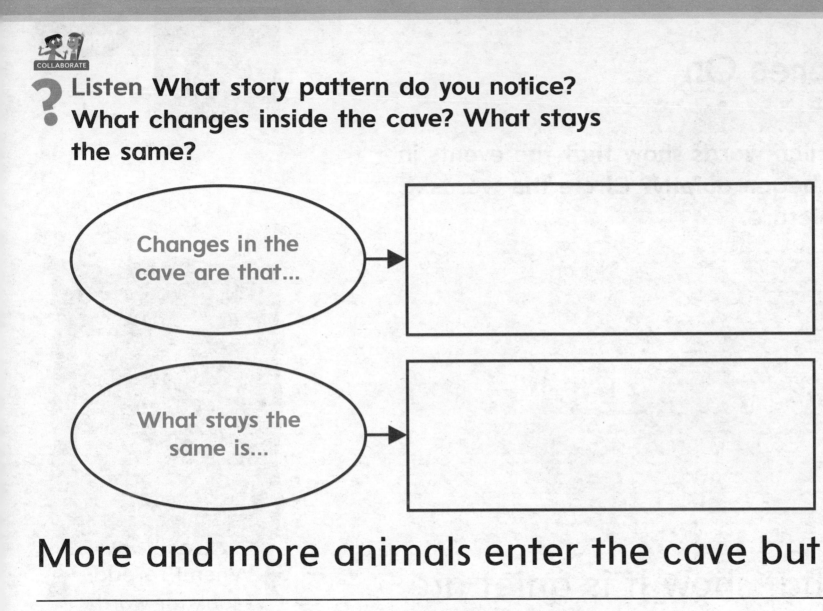

Changes in the cave are that...

What stays the same is...

More and more animals enter the cave but

_____

- -

_____

"Animal Homes"

COLLABORATE

? **Make Connections** Which two habitats are in the ground? Circle them. Draw a habitat that is on the water.

burrow

den

lodge

reef

A fish lives in a

Integrate

Look What can you learn from the photo about where meerkats live? Circle the clues.

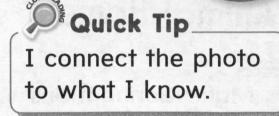

Quick Tip

I connect the photo to what I know.

A meerkat mother and pup looking out of their burrow.

Jonathan Heger/E+/Getty Images

Meerkats live

_____

- -

_____

Read Together

CLOSE READING

COLLABORATE

84 Unit 7 • Week 3 • Animal Habitats

When Daddy's Truck Picks Me Up

COLLABORATE

? **Look** How do the author and illustrator help tell how the boy feels? Write or draw clues.

Literature Big Book

Read Together

SazzyB/iStock/Getty Images Plus/Getty Images

The boy feels

_____

- - - - - - - - - - - - - - - - - - -

_____

CLOSE READING

Tip of the Week

Amy

When I **reread**, I look for clues about how the characters feel.

COLLABORATE

? Look Why did the illustrator place the words the way she did? Draw what they tell about.

The illustrator wanted to show

_____

- -

_____

"From Here to There"

? **Find Clues** How does the author help you know this page is about the past? Circle the clues.

Long Ago

Many years ago, people traveled in stagecoaches pulled by horses. The trip was slow and uncomfortable.

The author is telling us about the past because

_____

- -

_____

COLLABORATE

Look Tell a partner if this train is from today or long ago. Circle clues. Write words about it.

CLOSE READING
Quick Tip
I use photo clues and what I know.

A fast Japanese train waits at a platform.

Ingram Publishing

This train is

Ana Goes to Washington, D.C.

COLLABORATE

? **Look** Why does the illustrator include photos in the map? Circle yes or no for each question.

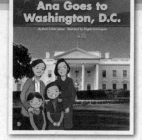
Literature Big Book

1. Do the photos show that the places are real? **yes** **no**

2. Do the photos show what the places look like? **yes** **no**

3. Do the photos show us where Ana lives? **yes** **no**

4. Do the photos show us where Ana is? **yes** **no**

The photos in the map show

_____

- - - - - - - - - - - - - - - - -

_____

CLOSE READING

Tip of the Week

John

When I **reread**, I use the pictures to help me understand.

Jetta Productions/Blend Images/Getty Images Plus/Getty Images

COLLABORATE

? Listen What is real and what is make-believe?
? Draw it.

Real	Make-believe

The photographs are

The people are

"See Our Country"

COLLABORATE

? **Find Clues** What helps you learn about animals that live in the Everglades? Circle the clues.

The Great Blue Heron lives in the Everglades.

The alligator lives in the Everglades, too.

I learn more by

_____

- -

_____

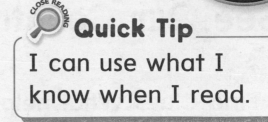

Listen The flag is a symbol of our country. What does the nursery rhyme say to do when the flag goes by? Talk about it with a partner. Underline clues.

Quick Tip

I can use what I know when I read.

The Flag Goes By

Hats off!
Along the street there comes
A blare of bugles, a ruffle of drums,
A flash of color beneath the sky:
Hats off!
The flag is passing by!

Pixtal/AGE Fotostock

When the flag goes by

_____

- -

_____

Bringing Down the Moon

COLLABORATE

? **Look** What do the words *Oh! Eeek! Ouch! Ooh!* and *Splash!* tell you? Draw and label it.

Literature Big Book

FogStock/Alamy

The sound words tell

_____

- -

_____

CLOSE READING

Tip of the Week

Eléna

When I reread, I look carefully at the words.

? **Look** **What really happened to the moon? Talk about the picture with a partner. Draw it.**

The moon

- - - - - - - - - - - - - - - -

"Day and Night Sky"

COLLABORATE

? **Find Clues** How does the Sun look like a giant fireball? Underline clues in the text. Circle a clue in the photograph.

Daytime

The Sun is very hot and bright. It looks like a giant fireball.

The Sun and a giant fireball are both

_____

- - - - - - - - - - - - - - - - - - -

_____

Giorgio Fochesato/E+/Getty Images

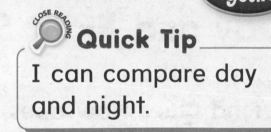

Look What do you see in the night sky? Circle it. Then draw how the sky looks in the daytime.

Quick Tip
CLOSE READING
I can compare day and night.

Fuse/Getty Images

In the night sky you can see

_____

- -

_____

Peter's Chair

COLLABORATE

? Look What clues help you know how Peter feels? Draw and write clues.

©Blend Images/Alamy

Text Clues	Picture Clues

Peter feels

_____

- -

_____

Read Together

EZRA JACK KEATS
PETER'S CHAIR

Literature Big Book

CLOSE READING

Tip of the Week

Marta

When I reread, I use pictures and text to know how characters feel.

Listen Which things are important to Peter?
Draw and label them.

One of Peter's favorite things is his

_____

- -

_____

Read Together

"The Clean Up!"

COLLABORATE

? **Find Clues** How do Dad's feelings change on these pages? How do you know? Circle clues.

Dad feels

Now Dad feels

Integrate

Listen How is the ending of Little Red Hen's song different from *Peter's Chair*? Circle clues that tell if the Little Red Hen got help.

Quick Tip
I compare the song and the story.

Song of the Little Red Hen

Who will help me plant some grains of wheat?
"Not I!" said her friend, the big white goose!
"Not I!" said her friend, the fat gray rat!
"Then I will do it myself!" said the Little
   Red Hen.

And so she did!

Pixtal/age fotostock

Little Red Hen's friends

- -

Hen Hears Gossip

? Listen What does Duck think the gossip is?
Draw it.

Literature Big Book

Each animal hears

_____

- -

_____

CLOSE READING

Tip of the Week

Jerome

I look for what the characters say when I **reread**.

COLLABORATE

? **Listen** What does Goose tell Turkey? What does Turkey tell Hen? Draw the pictures.

Goose	Turkey

Each animal heard

_____

- -

_____

Read Together

"Team Up to Clean Up"

COLLABORATE

? **Find Clues** How do the children feel about cleaning up? Underline a clue in the text. Circle clues in the photograph.

We plant a tree.

We took responsibility for making our neighborhood an even better place!

We did a good job!

The children feel

_____

- -

_____

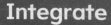

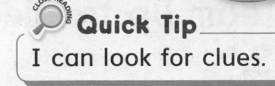
Look Look at the picture. How did Paul Revere tell citizens the British were coming? Circle clues.

CLOSE READING
Quick Tip
I can look for clues.

Paul Revere lived more than 200 years ago. He warned his town that British soldiers were coming.

Good citizens take care of

_____

- -

National Archives and Records Administration (NWDNS-208-PS-3200-5)

Bread Comes to Life

COLLABORATE

? **Look** How does the author make the text and photographs fun? Draw or write clues.

Literature Big Book

The author makes them fun by

_____

- -

_____

CLOSE READING

Tip of the Week

Ahmed

When I **reread**, I look for clues in the photographs and text.

Listen Which words help you know what the wheat is like? Draw the wheat and use a word to label it.

The wheat looks like

_____

- -

_____

Reread

"Nature Artists"

COLLABORATE

? Find Clues How does the author use photographs to teach you more about basket weaving? Circle clues.

I learned that

_____

- -

_____

COLLABORATE

Look **Draw and label one thing from nature that was used to build the log cabin in the photo.**

CLOSE READING
Quick Tip
I can look for clues.

This log cabin is in Columa, California.

We use natural resources to build

_____

- -

What's the Big Idea, Molly?

COLLABORATE

? **Listen** What do you picture about the place where the animals will get their ideas? Draw it.

Literature Big Book

The animals get their ideas

_____

- -

_____

CLOSE READING

Tip of the Week

Robert

When I **reread**, I picture in my mind what the text tells me.

COLLABORATE

Read Together

? **Listen** How does the author help you understand what happens when we work together? Write the clues.

Text clues	Picture Clues

When we work together

_____

- -

_____

"The Variety Show"

COLLABORATE

? **Find Clues** What is the problem? What is the solution? Circle clues.

I vote for dancing!

I vote for acting!

I vote for singing!

Mrs. Lopez, I have another idea!

Let's put on a variety show with dancing, singing, and acting.

Great! We can all work together.

Look at all the hands! The variety show wins!

Problem: Everyone wants to

_____

- - - - - - - - - - - - - -

_____

Solution: The problem is solved because

_____

- - - - - - - - - - - - - -

_____

COLLABORATE

Look How do these swimmers work together? Talk about it with a partner. Draw the shape the swimmers make.

CLOSE READING
Quick Tip
I can connect ideas.

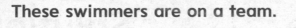
These swimmers are on a team.

When we work together, we

_____

- -

_____

All Kinds of Families!

COLLABORATE

? **Look** What makes a family? Draw and label a family.

Literature Big Book

CLOSE READING

Tip of the Week

Nina

When I **reread**, I use details to help me understand.

A family is made up of

_____

- -

_____

COLLABORATE

? Listen Which words help make the story fun?
Draw and label a picture of three fun families.

An author can make a story fun by

_____

- -

_____

"Good for You"

COLLABORATE

? Find Clues How does the author help you learn about foods to eat? Circle the clues.

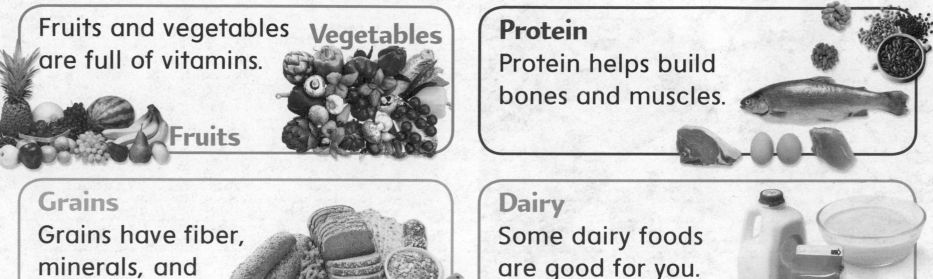

Fruits and vegetables are full of vitamins.

Vegetables

Fruits

Protein Protein helps build bones and muscles.

Grains Grains have fiber, minerals, and vitamins.

Dairy Some dairy foods are good for you.

A healthy diet includes

_____

- -

_____

COLLABORATE

Look Look at the items in the photo. Think about *All Kinds of Families*. What name could you give this family? Write a caption next to the photo.

Quick Tip
I think about things that go together.

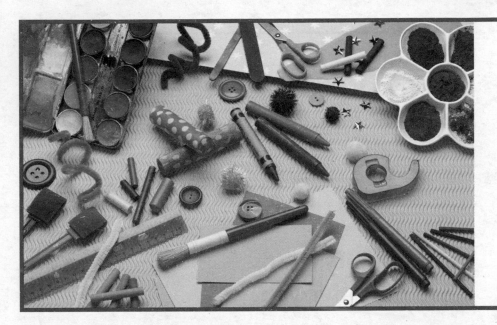

These things are a family because

_____

- -

_____

Panda Kindergarten

COLLABORATE

? **Look** How do the photographs help you know how people care for pandas? Draw it.

Literature Big Book

CLOSE READING

Tip of the Week

Dan

I look for clues in the photographs when I **reread**.

People care for pandas by

_____

- -

_____

Read Together

? **Look** What can you learn from the photographs?
What can you learn from the text? Write it.

Photographs	Text

Pandas learn

_____

- -

_____

"Saving Big Blue!"

? **Listen** What clues does the author give to help you figure out what a fluke is? Circle clues.

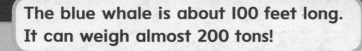

The blue whale is about 100 feet long. It can weigh almost 200 tons!

Each part of a blue whale's tail is called a *fluke*.

A fluke is

_____

- -

_____

COLLABORATE

Listen Where does the robin go to stay warm?
Underline the answer.

Quick Tip
I can reread to look
for details.

The Robin

The north wind doth blow,
And we shall have snow,
And what will poor robin do then,
Poor thing?

He'll sit in a barn,
And keep himself warm,
And hide his head under his wing,
Poor thing!

Liam Douglas

Birds can get warm in a

_____

- -

_____